AWAKENING MELA

Gathering Bone and Spirit to Light the Flame

Debi Vance Skaff
poems

Awakening Mela:
Gathering Bone and Spirit to Light the Flame

Copyright © 2025 by Debra S. Vance

All rights reserved. No part of this publication may be reproduced, distributed or transmitted in any form or by any means—including photocopying, recording, other electronic or mechanical methods, or by any information storage and retrieval system, without the prior written permission of the publisher.

ISBN: 979-8-218-59517-3
Published by Debra S. Vance, 2025.
United States of America

CREDITS
Cover Art:
Ichetucknee Springs, oil on canvas, by Debi Vance Skaff
Image taken by Sara Chesser
Graphic design and publishing support by Aliye Cullu

"Let yourself become living poetry."
~Rumi

For my husband and mother
Who continue to show me how to love.

CONTENTS

Light Prevails 1
The Seer 2
I Am the Water I Am the Sky 3
My Gift 4
Collective Grief 6
Force of Love 8
Council Oaks 9
Pious Spirituality 10
Wholeness 11
Sacred 12
Boundless. 14
Gratitude 15
We Were Born for This Time 16
Anam Cara. 18
Snakeskin. 19
I Love My Thighs 20
Altar of Being. 22
The Dreamer 23
This Time. 24
In Full Bloom. 26
Prepared to Fly. 28
Curious 29

Eclipse	30
Swallowing My Power	31
Grandmother	32
To Be Loved	34
Decoy	35
Locksmith	36
Ocean of Humanness	37
Always Here	38
Gift of the Ground	39
Ready to Fly	40
Love Prevailed	41
I Choose	42
I Am Learning How to Be an Old Woman	43
The Path	44
Meet Yourself	46
Pure Love	47
Full Moon Mantra	48
The Masterpiece	50
Peace	51
The Sacred River	52
The Art of Love	53
Beware the Rebellious Woman	54
The Calling	56
Fruit Salad Sangha	57
Sailing	58

PREFACE

My journey to awakening holds the tension of wanting to be both "something" and "no thing." Throughout my life I have endeavored to express my authentic self, while also following the spark of the Eternal, which I recognized early in childhood.

I have sporadically written poetry since I was young. As my corporate career came to a close, the urge to write emerged once again. The poems gathered in this book were mostly written since I retired. They nod to my process of creating and healing the "something," then letting it all go in surrender to the Divine, from which we all arise.

Whether you read sequentially, or let your intuition guide you to a page, may your reading of these poems kindle the eternal flame of Sacredness within you.

Note:
Mela is a Sanskit word meaning "gathering" or "to meet." It is also my crone name, given to me in my 60th year.

Light Prevails

On this sultry summer evening
the full moon bathes my garden
in a shaft of silver light
Reflecting the luminosity of the sun
upon my suburban temple
to remind me
that even in the dark of night
Light prevails

The Seer

I see with the innocent eyes of the infant
gazing in wonder at a new world

I see with the joyful eyes of the child
playing pretend with her dolls

I see with the passionate eyes of the maiden
discovering her divine feminine

I see with the loving eyes of the mother
nurturing life in all creatures

I see with the wise eyes of the crone
celebrating the season of winter

I see with the eyes of the Eternal Seer
accepting all in radiant light

I Am the Water I Am the Sky

On a June night
I step into my tepid pool
Stark naked floating on my back
Ears submerged
all I hear is my breath
Suspended
all I see are stars
and suddenly
I know I am not alone
I Am the water
I Am the sky

My Gift

You did not recognize my gift
of love
You took it as your due
Like a blue ribbon symbol of your worthiness
Never feeling its fragility
Never knowing its rarity
Never sharing its beauty
Just taking it

And you thought once won
It was yours
To place on your trophy shelf
Where it would stand waiting for you
To take down and admire
Then return to its proper place
Until next time
You needed to stroke the memory of your conquest

But my gift cannot live on your shelf
Of victories
Never feeling a caress
Never knowing honor
Never sharing a heart
Kept without essence

And one day
In need of your worthiness
You will reach to the shelf
Anticipating fulfillment
And find to your surprise
You have won
Only the dustless space
Where my gift once was

Collective Grief

It seems as if all of humanity
is engaged in a primal scream
We wage war upon ourselves
to express rage and sorrow
Cutting ourselves in a failed attempt
to ease our suffering
Indulging in substances with the illusion
that more
will soothe our torment.

When will we learn that what we are feeling
is referred pain?
Originating in our collective grief
A knowing without naming
that something is lost
or forgotten
That there must be more
than these separate selves roaming this planet

When we turn and face our grief
we can remember
that the cells in our bones
contain the trees, animals and ancestors
which have come before us.
We can remember
that the spark of light
animating our bodies
is the Divine expressing itself in us.

We can remember
We are Earth
We are Light
We are One

Force of Love

In quiet stillness I notice
the force of Love
Carrying me home

Council Oaks

Before community centers
and courthouses
We would gather under the council oaks
To decide our fates

Spreading ourselves
like acorns
Under the shelter
of ancient limbs

Resting atop deep roots
to soak in nature's knowledge
Trusting
In the wisdom of the Earth

Pious Spirituality

Pious spirituality
reeks of insincerity
Give me raw humanity
in all its flawed complexity

Wholeness

This universal urge
This ache for Oneness
is so powerful
pulling disparate worlds

Closer and closer
Faster and faster
toward each other
For an inevitable collision

and perhaps
after the smoke clears
we will see that it wasn't a collision after all
But a climactic merging
into Wholeness
and finally
We will know Peace

Sacred

I cannot remember
A specific moment
when I awoke as Consciousness

It wasn't at a retreat
or on my meditation cushion
or kayaking the gentle rivers
of my beloved home state

Not that these weren't
steps along the way

But one day
I realized I had taken a new shape
Bigger
Permeable
Formless

And I knew my life
And yours
As a sacred manifestation upon this Earth
And I was at Peace

Boundless

When the Boundless speaks
The words arise within me
Not from me

Gratitude

With heart in my hands
I go down on bended knee
Offering gratitude

We Were Born for This Time

I thought I knew
what the final journey
looked like
I've traveled the same path
so many times I can
do it without thought
Without awareness.

But suddenly it's dark
and a raging storm has blown through
toppling trees onto roads I've
traveled for decades
Challenging me to pay attention
Do I climb over or back up
to find a new path?

There are no more familiar landmarks
to guide my way
Only fallen debris
locked gates
dead ends
Now I must rely on a deeper knowing
An inner GPS
To navigate this new landscape

History has traveled
unknown paths before
And we fragile and determined
humans have always
Found the way
With Love
Connection
Community

We were born for this time

Anam Cara

My journey has been blessed
with soul companions
Connections that transcend this life
Those friends who awaken in me
my authentic feral nature
Who encourage me to stretch beyond
the tamed and controlled conventions
of our time
To connect with the wild potential
beating in my heart
Who dance with me
who enter deep waters holding my hand
who hear my darkest confessions
and love me anyway
Whose divine light joins with mine
creating bursts of radiance
for all the world to see

Snakeskin

Snake sheds old skin
upon life's thorns and branches
Leaving wounds behind

I Love My Thighs

I'm not exactly sure when
I started to love my thighs
In my shorts-avoiding teens
I hated every lump
every jiggle

Then somewhere between
middle and old age
I looked down
and instead of superficial flaws
I saw enduring strength and flexibility
Ignoring my youthful derision
my femurs, quads and hamstrings
have worked together
to carry me on this journey

So today
I honor them with above-the-knee dresses
and thrift store bathing suits
in the hopes they can feel
my awe
and gratitude

Altar of Being

When I am suffering
or indecisive
I return to my altar of Being
The anvil of my soul
against which everything
is hammered and shaped
Into my authentic truth

The Dreamer

Step back and notice
All that is and will be
Is dreaming the dreamer

This Time

Sometimes
When I'm very quiet
it all seems so familiar
as if we are in
an historical reenactment.

This time I'll hurt you
This time you'll abandon me

There's a park
near my house
a preserved 1800s farm.
The people who work there
dress in period clothing
and milk cows
and churn butter.
Perhaps we've agreed to meet again

This time I'll wear the soldier's uniform
This time you'll wear the farmer's overalls.

Over and over
we are actors in the same play
But in different roles

This time I'm the mother
This time you're the child

Until we finally know ourselves as One
and this time
We can rest.

In Full Bloom

I've grown weary
of vapid spirituality
The empty promise of
magical phenomenon and
manifestation
Balancing my chakras and
chanting have not led me
To the Divine

Like religious dogma, perhaps
these were needed steps
along the path
I don't know when they
Became distractions, but
One day
In a moment of deep quiet
I noticed a gleam in my being
and I knew God was in my very breath

These days I tend to
my garden of Stillness
Pruning sprouts of worry and resistance
Digging weeds of mindless doing
Fertilizing with awareness
to encourage bountiful growth
Knowing that my garden
is already in full Bloom

Prepared to Fly

Like the caterpillar
I've surrendered everything
to the chrysalis
I'm ready to emerge
colorful wings
fully extended
prepared to fly

Curious

Quietly curious
I inquire within.
What is this energy
which flows through me?
Patiently pulsing, then
reaching out
at just the right moment
to offer Itself

Eclipse

We pause in awe
to witness the brief merging of sun and moon
Feeling our insignificance, yet knowing
planets, stars, and even our small organic selves
all arise from the same source
And we are that Source

Swallowing My Power

I told myself
that I struggled with emotional eating
Soothing my sorrows in
comfort food
And after many years
the ache in my soul
became so unbearable
that I started to listen deeply
To my inner source of justice
To my body's impulse for right action
Honoring the very ground
of my being
And I realized
that all those years
I wasn't swallowing
my pain
I was swallowing my power

Grandmother

My grandmother was gifted
with needle and thread
She had the skill and flair
to turn the most ordinary household item
into high art
Finely embroidered pillowcases
tatted with lace trim
Intricately patterned quilts
lovingly stitched from simple muslin
and worn clothes
Even the sacks that held animal feed
became dresses or dish towels
gathered and smocked
for beauty and resiliency

I sometimes wonder
If we have lost our ability
 to see the blessings in the mundane
the potential in the cast off

Or perhaps we just stopped believing
In our own power
to transform

To Be Loved

As a young woman
I was easily seduced by sentiment
Falling at the feet
of any man who gave me
flowers, jewelry or chocolate
(especially chocolate)
Lovely offerings to be sure

But these days
My heart melts
When he insists on checking my oil
Picking up a prescription
and serving
my morning coffee in bed
Now I truly know
What it is to be loved

Decoy

My mind offers a thought
like a decoy
Luring me away
to plan
to worry
to ruminate
And for a brief moment
I ride the thought
until I remember
my thoughts
Are not who I Am

Locksmith

My shadows hide
in the farthest corners
of a steel vault
With double thick walls
and a heavy door
Secured by a combination lock
so complex that
my shadows feel safe
in their dark den

Until the locksmith arrives
with a master key
A lantern
held high
incandescent and radiant.
And what was once a safe refuge
is now a cage
with no escape
from the Light of Grace

Ocean of Humanness

I used to feel alone in a crowd
As if sheer numbers
created a wall around my heart
Locking me in
envious
confused
separate

Now I notice when I am with others
I am merging into an ocean of humanness
Both giving and receiving
Alive
Grateful
One

Always Here

It might appear
I rove aimlessly
Emptied, I place each foot
where my foot is called to be
Wandering, but not lost
somehow always Here

Gift of the Ground

Life takes its swings
throws its punches
From out of nowhere
Knocking me
to the ground
I struggle to rise
then realize
Why resist?
If I must be on the ground
perhaps here too
is something for me to learn
to embrace, or maybe
just to rest

Ready to Fly

The glider pilot
leaps off the side of the mountain
ready to fly with the wind
Not against it
Knowing that turbulence will happen
Determined to enjoy the ride
for as long as wind and gravity
will allow

Love Prevailed

Some people awaken
in a titanic shift
As if a lightning bolt
strikes from the sky
and from then on
they are lit from within

But for me
there was no bolt of lightening
Just small, electric moments
of knowing myself as Love
Then life's distractions
Then Love
Until slowly
The distractions became fewer
And Love prevailed

I Choose

Suffering in silence
Blood and bone whisper
What I don't change
I choose

I Am Learning How to Be an Old Woman

I am learning how to Be an old woman
Letting go of residual urges
to please
to attract
to be nice
to be anything other
than my saucy self
…when sauciness is called for

I am learning to die
So I can fully live

The Path

This journey to awakening
is not for the faint-hearted
I started slowly with a heavy load
Carrying my fears and feelings
upon my back
Afraid to go anywhere without them.
But as I struggled along the trail
each step forced me to leave something behind
My sadness now lies in the dust
my resistance, in the grass
I left my grief on a boulder
and my fear of being too much, under a tree

One by one
Step by step
my load has lightened
my pace quickened
I'm not sure where this path is taking me
I do know
I will arrive unburdened
Free

Meet Yourself

Enter in silence
Slip off your shoes, meet yourself
With deep reverence

Pure Love

Living from the Boundless
does not mean we become nicer people
We no longer need to be nice
to please others
to get our needs met
to follow the rules.
When niceness arises
It is without story
It is pure Love

Full Moon Mantra

I feel the fullness of this moon
offering its beauty
its radiant light
Signaling the end of something
Inviting me to let go
of what no longer serves

I feel the fullness of this moon
offering its beauty
Its radiant light
Signaling the end of something
Inviting me to let go
of what no longer serves

I feel the fullness of this moon
offering its beauty
its radiant light
Signaling the end of something
Inviting me to let go
of what no longer serves

…With Gratitude and Love

The Masterpiece

Nature continually practices the art of impermanence
Painting a new landscape
Drawing a beach
Sculpting a mountain
Then wiping the canvas clean
to start again

I grieve all that we've lost and for all who are suffering
Surrendered to our transience
With love and faith
That this beautiful process
 Is the Masterpiece

Peace

Peace demands no price
It can't be bought or bartered
It is the Love that we are

The Sacred River

The sacred river
calls me to its tannic waters
Offering its gentle current
to carry away my sorrow
Its bubbling springs
to cleanse my soul
Releasing my spirit
to merge with the ether
beyond the blue June sky.

The Art of Love

She painted over pain
offering sunny yellow
as if warm hues could
cover sad walls
Perhaps the paint itself
Is not meant to heal
Perhaps the painter
Is brushing Her radiance
into the darkest corners
Spraying Her light upon grief
Healing with the art of Love

Beware The Rebellious Woman

Beware the rebellious woman
no longer constrained
by the guardrails of youth

Beware the rebellious woman
whose mouth can soothe a troubled infant
and speak truth to a tyrant

Beware the rebellious woman
whose hands can create a masterpiece
and demolish the obsolete
all in one afternoon

Beware the rebellious woman
Whose mind no longer seeks data
but accesses the wisdom of the ages

Beware the rebellious woman
who has died the deathless death
and been reborn

For this moment.

The Calling

There is a calling within
First a whisper
Then an invitation
And finally, a hard shove
Dropping me to my knees

At some point I realize
I am not in charge
When the daughter is called
The daughter arises
When the teacher is called
The teacher arises
And when the poet is called
The poet arises
I am merely the vessel
Surrendered to the call

Fruit Salad Sangha

I love strawberries
Sweet, red lusciousness upon my tongue
Crisp apples with a hint of tart
excite my taste buds
The burst of goodness of a perfect blueberry
fills my mouth with joy
And there is nothing like
a juicy pink watermelon to quench my thirst
In the heat of summer

But a fruit salad has a special magic
where all the flavors and textures meet.
Mingling
Enhancing each other
Creating a unique and flavorful
culinary experience
that no single fruit
alone can achieve

Sailing

Until recently
I've lived my life as
a speedboat
Plowing through waves
Ignoring inconvenient winds
in pursuit of a distant
port of happiness

Now
I prefer living as
a sailboat
Embracing each wave
as essential
with faith that the winds
will carry me through
whatever remains of my
amazing imperfect life

Acknowledgments

To my dearest friend, Maureen Morehouse, who helped me rediscover my inner poet by challenging me to write every day when I retired. Without you, this book would not have happened. For my friend and teacher, Lissa Friedman, who allowed me to draft her as she took the headwinds on this life's spiritual journey, and whose love and wisdom continues to nourish my soul. For my Anam Caras, my soul friends: Andrea Easler, Jamie Duca Wilson, Erin Wallace, Penny Shaw Bugos and Elizabeth Paulson, who joyfully enter deep waters with me and love me no matter what.

For the wise, talented and creative Mary Bast, who encouraged me to enter my first poetry contest and who gave her precious time and feedback on early versions of this book.

For the members of the Awakening Mela meditation group whose presence and practice remind each of us we are Consciousness itself. Namasté.

As I sat to write this section, my heart opened in awe and gratitude for the many people I am blessed to travel this journey with. I love you.

www.ingramcontent.com/pod-product-compliance
Lightning Source LLC
LaVergne TN
LVHW051201080426
835508LV00021B/2733